An Unnecessary Breakdown Within Your Relationship

Communication Is Key

Taynia A. Coleman

www.tayniacoleman.com

Destined With A Purpose

Detroit, Michigan

2018

Copyright © 2017-2018

By **Taynia A. Coleman**

ISBN-13: 978-0692089736

ISBN-10: 069208973X

Publisher: Destined With A Purpose

tayniacoleman@gmail.com

www.tayniacoleman.com

ALL RIGHTS RESERVED.

This book contains material protected under International and Federal Copyright Laws and Treaties. Any unauthorized reprint or use of this material is prohibited. No part of this document may be reproduced or transmitted in any form or by any means, electronics, mechanical, photocopying, recording, or otherwise, without prior written permission of Taynia A. Coleman, and or Destined With A Purpose.

Dedication

Christian, April and Lauren my three heartbeats, thank you for always loving me unconditionally. I want you to know that if you don't stand for something, it is guaranteed that you will fall for anything, never fall. Never settle because there is so much more to life than the basics. Dig deep and blossom into this world full force.

To my love, you are the love of my life. God's mercy, His grace, and you are the reason that I feel and believe again. You are the reason that I am able to love again . . . I just want to say thank you, baby.

You brought me sunshine
When I only saw rain.
You brought me laughter
When I only felt pain.
—Donna Donathan

Acknowledgments

I would like to thank my family for always being there for me no matter the time, nor the hour. You are the real MVP's and I sincerely thank you. I would like to thank you, sister Tanikka Coleman for always making sure I am staying on task with my writings and readings. I love all of my siblings! You keep me on my toes at all times. I would also like to thank my father Roderick Gillison Sr and my mother Mablene Gillison for always keeping it real with me (straight no chaser). It never matters if I am right or wrong, all that matters is the truth. I say thanks a million for never turning your backs on me even in my darkest seasons you were always there and always there to bring me back to the light. I am truly humbled and blessed to have you all in my life. Again, I say thank you to the best part of me my children and my fiancé who pushes me even when I fight it. There were many times I was ready to throw in the towel but I didn't because I know this is God! God Bless!

TABLE OF CONTENTS

INTRODUCTION 1
CHAPTER 1 4
    RELATIONSHIP READY 4
    PRAYER 9
CHAPTER 2 10
    GROWING STAGES 10
    PRAYER 13
CHAPTER 3 14
    DIFFERENT STAGES IN A RELATIONSHIP 14
    PRAYER 18
CHAPTER 4 19
    COMMUNICATING WITH LOVE 19
    PRAYER 23
CHAPTER 5 24
    THE UNIVERSAL LAW: KARMA 24
    PRAYER 28
CHAPTER 6 29
    WHAT IS SPACE IN A RELATIONSHIP 29
    PRAYER 32
CHAPTER 7 33
    VOWS: FOR BETTER OR FOR WORSE 33
    PRAYER 37
CHAPTER 8 38
    FORGIVENESS 38
    PRAYER 41
CONCLUSION 42
    PRAYER 45

INTRODUCTION

This book was written for all women that are in any stage of a relationship. It was written to give you a reset in your relationship; a reset in your mind, if needed. It was written for those of us that are engaged and for those of us that are married. There are many different decision that we have to make in life for out happiness and most times something dramatic has to happen to get our attention. Sometimes we hit a bump in the road, and we do not always know how to get around it. We do not know which way to go or which way to turn, but the solution could be as simple as opening your mouth and expressing yourself with patience and love. It is time to stop holding everything in because your mate cannot understand what you need without you letting it be known.

Communication is extremely important between couples; it is the key factor to a lasting relationship. Effective communication is imperative to run a household; communication is demanded in order to know what's going on in each other's lives from day to day. It's also essential to discuss any issues that need to be addressed, as well as, disclosing to your mate how you are feeling and if any feelings have changed, and vice versa. We are living in a world where things change all the time, change is inevitable. Therefore, it is important that we learn to open up and communicate effectively with our spouses.

More importantly, we need to learn how to pray for our men and how to pray for our relationships, while praying for ourselves. Prayer is imperative within your relationship and your home: pray for your husband/mate, yourself, and you both as a couple because it would be a long, hard road without God in the midst. Prayer holds things together; mixed with faith it can and will move mountains. However, we must remember that faith without works is dead; you must pray and do the work. Prayer is not a magic trick. You cannot just pray and expect for everything to fall into place at that particular moment. Sometimes God will send the right people, at the right time, in the midst of our storm, to help us out of trials and tribulations.

I hope you receive the information in this book and apply it to your relationship where needed. The prayers in this book are anointed and can be recited daily until you experience a breakthrough. In all, I pray that there is something that you learn and take away from this book; I pray that you are able to dig deep and pull through in order to make your relationship work!

Take notes and look within to see the changes that you need to make in your relationship. Most people change because they want more out of their lives; they know that there is better on the other side. If you trust the process and know that communication, trust, and honesty will help your relationship, then a deeper stronger love connection will be waiting for you.

Love is key because without love there would be no need to change anything, so it takes hard work, dedication, and most of all prayer to experience the best love from the one that is designed for you. Trust the process and trust God more than ever.

CHAPTER 1

RELATIONSHIP READY

To find out if you are truly ready for a relationship, or to figure out if the relationship that you are presently involved in is truly what you are ready for, ask yourself: Am I giving my best in my relationship, or am I holding back for some odd reason? Am I ready to give my all in a relationship? Can I handle what comes along with a relationship? Am I ready for love? Sometimes people hold back within their current relationship because they are afraid to love and get hurt, again. Holding on to a relationship that you are not sure if you really want but are too afraid to let the relationship go out of fear of being alone is not healthy. However, most people do not realize that they are holding back until it is a little too late.

Withholding from the relationship causes a complete disconnect; it causes you to not hear your partner's concerns, wants or needs. It puts a strain on the relationship which will indeed cause unnecessary stress to you and your partner. If you find yourself "loving" while holding back, or without giving your whole heart, it can become depressing and draining, especially if you really do see or desire a future with this person. If you do not want to lose him or her, you will need to step your game up by weeding out the negativity that is causing your fear. Fear can have a serious grip on you if you are not able to get a hold of it and cancel it out of your life. In order to cancel out fear, the spirit of fear, say a quick spiritual warfare prayer such as "In the name of Jesus! I come against fear, I bind up being fearful in my life, I cancel it out now, and I loose the spirit of faith. I loose the spirit of bravery over my life and over my relationship. In Jesus mighty name I pray. Amen."

Being emotionally disconnected can be a major problem in any relationship. A relationship without emotions and real love is pointless. It will eventually lead to non-stop arguing, fighting and miscommunication on a daily basis. Take some time out to get your thoughts in order, process your feelings, and figure out why you are afraid to give it your all. Try to give the relationship a real chance 100% just take a real chance and let down your guard. Do not hold your current partner accountable for your past relationships that did not work out. It is not fair to hold all men accountable for what one man did to you because every man is not the same. Every man is not looking to hurt you. I know that it may sound cliché, but it is the truth. He is here to love you properly, like you are supposed to be loved, but only if you let him. Do not be afraid to love again, because if you allow yourself to love fully and completely it can unlock a love that you have never ever known. Remember that as much as you may want to believe that he should do all the work, he can't; it takes two people to make any relationship work.

Make a decision to love this man with 100% of you, meaning give him your all or nothing at all. Giving 50% of yourself is not fair for any relationship, and trust me you would not want half of any man. If you do not want to give your all, but you are expecting him to give his all, then it will never work because he will be lacking the love that he needs from you. Never lead anyone on, especially if you do not want to give him everything he needs. Take a self-inventory and figure out what it is that you want before wasting someone else's time and energy. Put yourself in his shoes; would you deal with someone that loves you only when it is convenient?

Would you love someone that can change their love for you within a blink of an eye, or would you want someone to love you unconditionally? Would you prefer someone to hold you down, or would you want someone to give up on you at every sign of trouble? Would you want someone to love you until you are whole again, or would you want someone to run away every time you cry out or have a concern?

The questions above are some questions that you should seriously consider before starting or continuing a relationship that you have doubts about. If you want a real relationship, and if you want someone to love you with 100% of themselves, then you must be ready and willing to give that same 100% back. I suggest that you lay everything out on the table with your significant other to make sure that you all understand what type of relationship you are committing to before anyone catches feelings (or the relationship gets more serious). Be open and honest with yourself as well as with your partner. Honesty should be your number one priority within any of your relationships.

Decide today that you will not continue to walk in your past. You want and need to start a new, revived and refreshed life. You need to overcome your pain and frustrations before starting or continuing a relationship and put the focus on you for a moment in order to become your best you. Otherwise, you will continue to operate in the same cycle from your past, causing nothing but self-hurt, doubt, pain and fear. Staying broken and acting as if you are healed will cause uncertainty and disbelief resulting in you believing that you are not capable of being loved the proper way; it will develop into trust issues if you continue this behavior. You will begin to doubt yourself and your relationship because you have allowed fear to set in. Instead, be bold and take a stand; take back your life!

Always go with the choice that scares you the most, because that's the one that is going to help you grow. —Caroline Myss

Take a risk on love and love again. Give him 100% of you, as you would expect the same from him. He could be just what you have been praying and asking God for, but how will you ever know if you do not take that chance? This relationship could be a blessing, so be careful not to block what God is doing.

Lastly, and most importantly, know what you want before dragging a person through an unwanted relationship. Nobody wants ANOTHER HEARTBREAK.

An Unnecessary Breakdown Within Your Relationship

PRAYER

Dear Heavenly Father, I am coming to you humbled with a broken heart and a broken spirit. I am asking you to take this pain away and fill this void in my heart, Lord. You said in your word that you are close to the brokenhearted, and I believe you because I know that you are near me. I am rebuking the spirit of fear, rejection and self-defeat in the mighty name of Jesus; they have no authority over me. God, I know you to be a healer and a mind regulator, and right now I am in need of your healing. I want to be whole and complete. Lord, I know that I am here to serve a purpose, so please use me as you will. In Jesus mighty name, I pray.

Amen

CHAPTER 2

GROWING STAGES

At the start of a relationship, everything is new and exciting. You take the time to find out what each other's likes and dislikes are; you find out who a person really is. After talking for a while, you find out that you guys have more in common than not in common. You begin to fall hard for one another, to the point that you both talk day and night and night and day. You begin to really like this person so much that you want to know everything about them, from their whereabouts to every thought. You become consumed with new love, and it becomes everything that you know. Now some time has passed, and you have begun to wonder if this will be the person you will spend your forever with. Everything is loving and wonderful, and then you guys start to evolve together. You are in love, in total bliss, until one day you want more out of life. Your thought process has changed, and you no longer desire the simple things in life; you no longer want to just be okay with whatever happens just happens.

You try to talk to your man and tell him the new things that are going on in your life; you try to tell him your new wants, needs and desires, dreams, and aspirations but he is not listening; he is not used to this new you. He does not know how to deal with this new situation, and it may take him some time to process it. He doesn't fully understand it. All the while inside, you begin to see that you no longer like what he likes. Your conversations are different. He feels as though you have changed, and he is right because you have; you are evolving into the real you. You have grown; you no longer want or desire what you used to want. You want more out of life, but he has grown content; he does not know anything but the old you.

What do you do? This is a good question because many relationships get stuck at this point and someone's pride eventually to gets hurt. Women and men change all the time; but, if you are going to stand the test of time, then you will need to grow TOGETHER. Give him the time he needs to get used to the new idea of how things are going to be. He may adjust to this new life and he may even want to improve some things about his life and you both as a couple as one. This could be a win, a win for you both individually and together as a couple.

Do not leave each other behind. Keep each other updated; talk about the hard stuff. Sit down and explain to him what you are feeling; share your thought process about the things you now want out of life. Eventually, he will begin to feel the same way, and maybe even want more out of life than you do. You may just boost his energy to create a better world for himself and for you. Vibe off of one another. He will always want to see you happy and winning. He will be able to stand by your side and hold you down. He should be your confidant when you need a breath of fresh air and to refocus on life; he should be there to push you and you do the same for him. This thing called life has its ups and downs but with each other you should go far in life. No one stays the same; change is inevitable on this life journey.

He should be evolving or wanting to evolve because he sees how much you have grown and have changed for the better. There is nothing greater than changing with the love of your life, wanting more out of life, and growing together as one. It is priceless!

No one stays the same; change is inevitable on this life journey.

Remember that if he is not happy with the change or even willing to adapt with you, then you may want to do some inventory. You both should be on the same page at the end of the day.

PRAYER

Father God, help us in this changing phase. Teach us how to grow as individuals and still grow together as a couple. Help us to communicate effectively. Let us learn to deal with different situations without fighting, but with a greater understanding. Give us the desire to want to learn each other, to learn from each other, and learn how to work out our issues and grow from them. Teach me to be who he needs me to be, and teach him to be who you have called him to be so that we can hear each other's needs and wants. Help me to be an open vessel. In Jesus name.

Amen

CHAPTER 3

DIFFERENT STAGES IN A RELATIONSHIP

The Good Times

Good times are always the best part of any and every relationship. Appreciating the good times in a relationship involves letting go and living in the moment. Do not hold on to the bad times; do not stay there. When things are going well, please do not wonder if it is too good to be true; you take the time to enjoy each other, love each other, and comfort one another. Loving each other is more than just words it is a lifestyle.

The fun times are the greatest of all time; it is a moment that you never want to end. Waking up in pure bliss because your heart is growing fonder of your relationship, falling in love over, and over again: texting and calling throughout the day to make sure he is not stressing at work; him checking on you because he misses you and vice versa. When in love you are excited to make it home from a long day of work to lay up under bae, cuddle, talk, kiss, and make sweet love. The sex is the bomb because the chemistry between you two is like fireworks. What can top this feeling? Absolutely nothing! There are no words that can describe this happy feeling in the air, nothing but love and happiness. Until . . .

The Bad Times

The bad times do not last long, but they do take a toll on your relationship and out on yourself. You lose focus on what is important and forget how to make your relationship work. The arguing is not as consistent as it would be in the "ugly times", but it is enough to make you wonder what is going on. Must we argue about the dumbest situations because someone is irritated about something, but don't know how to communicate or process their feelings so it it's taken out on the wrong person.

This is a phase of ups and downs; one-moment you all are cool, and the next, you are bickering for no real reason. It just seems like you may need a little "me time" to just clear your mind. Most of the time we bring home the frustrations of the world and drop them on our partner's lap without even knowing it. It is okay to let him know how your day went, but it is another thing to take out your anger on him because of something someone else did to you and vice versa. Home is supposed to be your happy place, where there is peace and serenity. If you feel that you do not have peace at home, then I would advise you two to come together and have a long talk (without fighting) to find out what issues are bothering you both. Lay it all out on the table without holding anything back. Work it all out; talk it all out. You can even pray it all out in order to bring peace back into the atmosphere. Where there is love, there is also peace—the very thing you will need to face the storms that lie ahead. Sometimes the storm can rock the boat a little too fast if we do not catch the waves.

The Ugly Times

The ugly times in a relationship will have you questioning your sanity. They are worse than the bad times. There is so much miscommunication that it will start to make you feel sick or even crazy. Most times you cannot fully get your point across because either it comes out wrong or it gets taken the wrong way. You begin to wonder: Is this even worth fighting for? What are we doing? What am I doing? Constantly arguing, unable to hear each other's concerns, wants, desires, or needs. On top of all of that, there is minimal to no sex; because of the loss of communication, there is no sex drive, there is only anger and frustration. If there is sex it is meaningless sex, which means you have sex and right after things go right back to the way they were. Not being able to see eye to eye has to be the absolute worse feeling of all time.

It is like no matter what you just cannot seem to get along. Every word, every thought, and every feeling become a fight. The disrespect and the dishonor is at an all-time high at this stage.

Your only focus is to hurt each other with your words and actions. Something has to give!

Now it is starting to affect your work, you are off, and everything feels like it is falling apart. This is a no-win-situation because your world is tumbling down. You begin to feel as if you cannot breathe because there is no peace in your home. Something must change, but you do not know what to change, or how to even change it. It is a struggle sometimes, but if your relationship is going to work, you both have to reconnect and do the work apart (working on self) as well as together (working on the relationship as a whole). You cannot work on the relationship if you do not have yourself aligned and balanced. Believe me, prayer does change things! This is not just a saying; this is real life. Instead of arguing go and pray and talk to God about it. Pray together; go to church together; turn your whole focus back on God and learn how to love each other the right way. God will lead you, but you have to be willing to follow. Marriage/pre-marital counseling will always help get the relationship headed in the right direction again.

Taynia A. Coleman

PRAYER

Lord, I am feeling so lost and alone. I need your strength in order to make it through. I don't want to fight and argue with my spouse anymore. God, please help this marriage; we are hurting. Place us back on good terms with one another. We are lacking love right now, and it's hard for me to function without it. Father, send help our way because we need it right now. Show us how to make it through this rough patch, together. Show us the proper way to love each other, and to be there for one another because it is important for to us. In Jesus mighty name, I pray.

Amen

CHAPTER 4

COMMUNICATING WITH LOVE

*C*ommunication is vital to any relationship; and, if it is lacking, your relationship is headed for danger. Communicate with your lover, and be open with your partner. This will allow the trust to set into your relationship and stay in your relationship. You want your mate to become your best friend, and you want to be someone he can trust and feel completely safe with. Opening up will make him trust you and tell you things that he has never told anyone; it will secure you and him, solidifying the trust inside of your relationship.

A relationship where you can sit for hours and talk about anything or be comfortable enough in each other's space for hours and talk about nothing is key to comfort. This is vital because without communication there is no true relationship. I know that sometimes it is hard for us as women to communicate, especially if we feel like no one is listening. This by itself can cause us to shut down internally, and it can make us start holding back things that, in fact, need to be said.

However, a key principle to live by is in Proverbs 15:8 (AMP): "A hot-tempered man stirs up strife, but he who is slow to anger appeases contention." First, we have to check our tone to make sure that we are not coming off as harsh. This in itself can and will start an uproar. Secondly, stay focused on one thing at a time; know what direction you want to go in order to have the proper conversation that's needed in order to push your relationship forward. The conversation of where you both decide on what is bothering you within your relationship the most, put it on the table, and deal with it. Do not go back and forth bringing up something so old that you both have forgotten and forgiven. Just let it go and talk about the real issues at hand.

Miscommunication comes into play when couples stop understanding each other. When a couple start to ignore each other feelings no one is really trying to hear the other person because no one is really listening; they are only trying to get their points across. Everyone is fighting to be heard, but no one is actually listening. This is where most relationships fail. All of the back and forth arguing brings about frustration and unhappiness and causes pure anger within the relationship. With all of the unnecessary kerfuffle, it is no surprise that miscommunication can cause heartbreak, anxiety, and distance.

While effective communication is the key to any healthy relationship, you must understand that it does take time, practice, and, most of all, having love for one another. James 1:19 (KJV) states: "Wherefore, my beloved brethren, let every man be swift to hear, slow to speak, slow to wrath." We have to learn our men and their body language; this includes when they want to talk and when they just want to be left alone. You never want to come across as a nag because this will, often times, make the man feel like, why bother? Always have a soft place for him, meaning that it is okay to be nice and loving. This will make him open up and keep the lines of communication open. Now, I am not saying that you will always agree with everything he has to say, but make him feel like he is heard because you are sincerely listening. Men need to feel like they are needed, wanted, respected and loved by their woman. Do not always respond without thinking and without hearing him out first. Be sure to respond because you have thought about your answer and you are sure that it is what you really want to say. Take a deep breath and breathe in order to stay calm during these trying times.

Trust me when I say that everything will not always be cookies and cream. You will indeed have your setbacks and mishaps. It comes with the package, but you must learn how to pick your battles wisely. Choose if the situation requires your energy or even your input. Every mistake or concern does not need your correction, sometimes it your stillness will calm the air, remember everything does not always have to be a big blow-up.

Communication works both ways, but remember that you teach people how you want to be treated. If he notices that you are not always yelling and screaming, then guess what? Eventually he will stop all the yelling and screaming because he will feel foolish being the only one to respond with negativity. Slowly but surely you guys will agree to stop fighting and work on the solution to your problems. Remember that there is a process in learning how NOT to blow up at the first sign of drama. It takes time for things to turn around, but if you keep working on it, it will eventually change for the better. No matter what it looks like, never give up. Change does not happen overnight.

When you are experiencing issues, it is best to always lay it all out on the table instead of holding it in. Meaning, have a mental list or even write out all of the issues you would like to discuss. Remember, the more you hold things in, the angrier you will become, and then you will be the one exploding and causing excess drama. I cannot express this enough you do not want to lose focus and make yourself sick on the inside; therefore, it is okay to discuss the issues and work on them. Holding it in will cause headaches, which can lead to illness physically and emotionally.

Ephesians 4:26 (AMP): "Be angry [at sin—at immorality, at injustice, at ungodly behavior], yet do not sin; do not let your anger [cause you shame, nor allow it to] last until the sun goes down." Meaning you can be angry and upset at the situation at hand, but do not stay that way. You have all day to be upset; but, by the end of the day, talk about it, let it go (truly let it go), and forgive. You do not have to carry all of that anger inside of you. Please just let it out, work on it, and move past it.

PRAYER

Father God, I am asking you to help me communicate within my relationship effectively; help me communicate with love, understanding and respect. As I want to be received with love, understanding and respect. I am asking for peace within myself and inside of our relationship, and peace within our home. Lord, help me to be slow to anger while trying to communicate effectively with my significant other. I want to keep an open dialog and be able to hear every word and take it into consideration. I want to feel safe and secure with my better half. I want to show love and be loved in every way. In Jesus mighty name.

Amen

CHAPTER 5

THE UNIVERSAL LAW: KARMA

When you are in a relationship, it is important to always put the person in your shoes before doing anything. Ask yourself: *How would I feel if he was to do that to me?* I believe that this key will keep your relationship 100% authentic. Keeping your significant other at the forefront of your mind at all times will keep you balanced, refreshed and renewed. If this is the person that you truly love and adore, then faithfulness and anything else should be easy to obtain. The unfaithfulness, lying and cheating that a lot of people go through in their relationships should be easy to avoid if you keep your partner at the forefront of your mind.

A woman's intuition is worth so much more than a man will ever understand.

Let's face it; what goes around comes around. It is in the Bible; it is a universal law. It is called sowing and reaping. According to Job 4:8 (KJV): "Even as I have seen, they that plow iniquity, and sow wickedness, reap the same." It is always important to do unto others as you would want them to do unto you. If you cannot imagine your man/woman out cheating on you, giving someone else what you feel belongs to you, then it is simple. Do not go out and give what is his/hers away to someone else that should never be allowed in this space.

No matter how many times a woman forgives her man, if he continues to do the same thing without any change, then eventually she is either going to A) leave him or B) start cheating right along with him (which is never good). Once this happens, it will only keep getting worse. If a person is this unhappy, then it makes no sense to stay in the relationship. Sit down, have a long conversation, and figure out if you two will continue to grow together or if you should go your own separate ways. As always, counseling is key in these type of situations because sometimes both of your thought processes can be cloudy and confusing because of all the tension and anger. Counseling is the best possible option and the most responsible one. It will help to open and close doors and situations that need to be discussed. It will cause you all to really work on your relationship. It is an option that everyone will be able to respect at the end of the day, especially if there are children involved.

A woman can only take so much . . .

In certain situations sometimes if a man would just take the time to listen to his woman, then she would tell him exactly what the issue is that she is having; but, he would have to be willing to listen and also willing to adjust. A woman, without a doubt, will tell a man when she has had enough and when she is completely done. When a man refuses to listen and continues to cheat on his spouse, it leaves her feeling lost, broken, confused and empty inside losing all hope. Who wants to continue to go through that, the answer is no one. It is a great deal of hurt on so many levels.

It may be difficult for her to advance at this point it will take a lot of will power and strength on the inside that she possibly hasn't found yet. She may eventually shut down; and, once she has shut down, there is no coming back because she has already come back too many times before, only to get hurt again. In her mind, she has determined that he had his chance to get it right, but did not take advantage of it. He did not choose her. As a result, she decides to leave him mentally.

In her mind, it is over, but she has not physically left the relationship yet. Once she leaves the relationship mentally, there is a 99.9% chance that she has another man or is thinking about it heavily. She will eventually act on her thoughts; and, once she does, it is a wrap because she has now turned into THE liar, cheater and deceiver. She will be in a place that she never thought was even possible.

Once the relationship has gone down this road, there is no need to even continue. When he finds out about his woman's infidelities, he is going to leave her without a doubt (most men do). A man cannot take the heartache, pain, rejection and confusion that comes along with being cheated on. His pride will not let him. He will not stick around and wait for a change, as long as a woman would in most cases.

Ladies, the best advice for when, or even if, your relationship takes a turn for the worse after you have given your all is that you must take a stand. The cheating will only continue to happen if you allow it to. It took a long time for me to learn this lesson because I could never understand what I needed to do as a woman. However, this does not have to be you. If you do not see progress and keep finding yourself in the same position time and time again, then you will need to take a bold step and be honest with yourself. Is this what you signed up for? Is this what you will continue to allow? Does this make you happy, or does it make you feel less than a woman? Could you share your man with another woman? Does he really love you? Do you love yourself to want better for yourself? Once you take the time to answer these questions, truthfully, you will have your answer. Honesty starts with yourself. It may be difficult at first, but it is something that you will need to do in order to stand as a woman, in order to stand on your own two feet again. No one ever deserves to be broken nor to stay that way.

Taynia A. Coleman

PRAYER

Lord, I need you! I am feeling lost and confused, and I need to re-examine my life. How did I get here? Lord, please help me put my significant other at the forefront of my mind at all times because I never want to hurt or lose him. I don't want to lose myself in this process either. Help me to see what's important, help me be the wife that he needs me to be, and also help him be the husband that I need him to be. I pray that we never lose trust in our relationship nor focus. This is the person that I want to love and honor and respect for the rest of my life. Lord, I am asking that the respect within our relationship never leaves because we love each other and honor each other. Send help our way. Help us be exactly what each other needs when we need it. In Jesus mighty name I pray.

Amen

CHAPTER 6

WHAT IS SPACE IN A RELATIONSHIP

When you are in a relationship, it is not good to attain, or make it a necessity to get, a large amount of space from your significant other. For example, you shouldn't need that let's take a break for a while and find ourselves type of space. You should not need this type of space within your relationship. It does not work like that. It should never exist in a marriage, an engagement, or any exclusive relationship.

What type of space is allowed within a relationship? If you ask me, the answer will always be: No space is allowed! Okay, maybe if some fresh air is needed or either he or she wants to go for a walk or take a ride to clear his or her mind; but, that is about it. I believe that when two people agree to walk together according to scripture, it means through the thick of things. They should be able to come together on misunderstandings and work them out, whatever the case may be. Leaving should never be an option unless you are leaving with no plans of returning.

Generally, when a couple separates, they give each other enough time and space for new buddies/friend, and cheating to creep in or, even worse, for hatred to begin to set in. It can also cause your spouse to feel rejected and neglected. If a person needs that much space and time, then maybe they no longer want to be involved and have a reservation on leaving anyway. Whatever the case may be, a person should always have respect for the other person, enough to be open and honest about their decisions and their thought process.

As always, transparency is the key; be as real with them as you would want them to be with you. I will say this a million times until I am blue in the face: communication is so vital in any relationship. You should be able to talk to one another about real feelings and life choices. If your feelings have changed within your relationship, then you need to have a serious talk. You could learn that maybe the issue is something that your significant other had not noticed before, but will make an effort to change in the future. Some things need to be talked about instead of being allowed to dwell inside of your head.

Change is inevitable, do not be afraid if you have changed; this is something that will need to be addressed as well. Never believe that a person automatically knows what you want and/or desire because that will always cause disappointment in the end. It is impossible for someone to know what your thoughts are even if you have been together for 20-30 years. If communication is not present inside of your relationship, then I would like to suggest counseling or seeking a relationship coach/expert in order to catch the breakdown and to help solve the problem. As always you should continue to pray, seek and find God in all that you do.

Taynia A. Coleman

PRAYER

Father God, I ask you to show us the way to communicate with understanding and not with frustration. Show us how to communicate and find the solution to the problem instead of arguing out of anger and not listening to one another. I ask that you open our hearts and our minds to walk on one accord. I ask that we be able to work out any situation, whether good or bad, that comes our way. Help us to stay grounded. In Jesus mighty name, I pray.

Amen.

CHAPTER 7

VOWS: FOR BETTER OR FOR WORSE

*E*veryone is all for a relationship when everything is smooth sailing. When the finances are just right, the bank account is tight, the children are healthy, and no one is arguing and fighting; just pure contentment. When life falls into place for us, we cannot help but to be on a natural high because there is no stress, no failure, no pain, no suffering and no tears; everything and everyone is all walking on one accord. As much as we would love for it to stay this way, unfortunately, life can happen at any moment. Life is a roller coaster ride of the ups and downs with a lot of back and forth: the tragedies, the attack on marriages and family, the silent drug problem, the alcohol addiction, the gambling, the lying, the cheating, the deceit, the children acting out, financial problems etc. it all can take place at any time in life. It all can fall apart at any moment if we let it sometimes the best thing to do is never give up hope. You may feel like you are at your lowest point in life but always remember that what you go through is only for a season. The silent struggles and the internal problems that no one knows about can become even bigger if we dwell there. You must get a hold of the issues and stop them in their tracks.

As I have mentioned before, change is inevitable there is no way around it. We have to learn to embrace it head-on. Therefore, it is important to stay prayerful and watchful while going through the good and the bad times. You never know when you will need one of those prayers to rely on for strength. However, troubles will not last always, and that is a promise.

The bad times within a marriage can take a toll on the entire household. The children can feel the effects, as well as the stress of an argument, and, more than likely, they will begin to act out. The first step is to try your best not to argue in front of the children; whatever it is should be discussed privately. Sometimes this can be the hardest thing to do when you have to get things off of your chest, but trust me there will be less confusion within the household.

Children should not hear every disagreement between you two. Only bring a situation to them after you and your significant other have come to a conclusion concerning them. By doing so, it will not make them feel as though they need to choose a side. Stability is the key to winning in this area if it is an area of concern. Children need stability and consistency in their lives. Relationships are a balancing act, especially when children are involved. Therefore, it is imperative to keep an open dialog to stay on track.

When people think about marriage, they think of all the pretty things, all the excitement and happiness; but, that is not all that marriage is. Facing those moments when the relationship is turned upside down will determine if you will stand the test of time. Being invested in your relationship only when everything is good, and not being present when it all goes down, shows that you are not truly dedicated. Let's really dig deep and think about this for a second. Do your vows mean anything to you at all, or did you just say them to walk down the aisle? As you consider what has been discussed, you will realize that it is very imperative to mean what you say and to say what you mean.

Get your vows out and think about what each statement means to you. Try to figure out if you are in this for the long run or just for the "good times" that do not last forever. Dig deep and figure out if you have your significant other's back if they fail to be whom you thought they were, or if they are struggling with something internally. Are you the person that they can trust, the person that will never leave their side? For better or for worse, do you really mean it? This is definitely something to think about. Make a decision to honor your vows and become the woman that you are supposed to be. Be loyal to your relationship and be loyal to yourself. Remember that prayer and communication are the keys to standing the test of time within any type of relationship. Instead of arguing go into your prayer closet and change the atmosphere inside of your home. Bring peace and calmness into the atmosphere and more than that bring love into it.

An Unnecessary Breakdown Within Your Relationship

PRAYER

Lord, I ask that you help me to forgive and never hold a grudge against my spouse. I know that I am not perfect, but I am willing to do my part in order for this to work. I pledged to be here for my husband, and he has pledged to be here for me. I am praying that we can make it out of any situation and be here for one another no matter what problem arises. I am here to learn from him and to grow with him, and I pray that he can learn from me and grow with me. He has been here for me, so Lord help me to be what he needs me to be. In Jesus mighty name.

Amen.

CHAPTER 8

FORGIVENESS

A relationship without trust is not really a relationship at all; you are just existing with one another. If there is not a level of trust, love, respect and understanding, then what is the point of wasting any time at all, right? A lot of worrying and wondering will be what comes of these types of relationships because all you will be concerned about is their whereabouts, and what they are doing at every moment of the day when you are not around.. For so long men and women stay stuck in empty relationships because the trust is so far gone that they do not know how to get it back.

Let me tell you, it takes a ton of work to trust again, but it all starts with forgiveness. In order to forgive someone, you have to first start with forgiving yourself in order to forgive the one who hurt you. This is the first step of healing and forgiveness.

Un-forgiveness brings about a burden in our lives, and it weighs heavily on our hearts. Often times, as women, we are hurt more than men because we wear our hearts on our sleeves. Once we decide to give away our hearts, we expect to be treated with love, loyalty and respect, but we do not always receive these things. That is the harsh reality of it all.

The pain, the hurt, the rejection, and the broken trust can linger on the inside for a long time if we are not careful. Within any relationship, we have our ups and downs, the good times as well as the bad. Let's face it; sometimes we even do things to hurt the ones we truly love. Quite often, we need forgiveness ourselves, which explains why it is imperative to keep our feelings and our better half's feelings at the top of our thoughts. Remember, they do not want to be hurt just like you do not want to be hurt.

Most of the time you can hold on to un-forgiveness without realizing it. Un-forgiveness can flare up if you think about the person and/or if you see the person. If you still become angry or upset, then un-forgiveness is still lingering. If seeing them or thinking about them puts you in a bad head space, then, let's be honest, you are still letting them control your space, time and energy. Do not give them that power. Do not give anyone that type of power over you it could be detrimental to your health.

Steps for true forgiveness would consist of first bridging the chasms within your relationship and to stop holding on to things that will not matter a month from now. It's time out for hovering emotions deep within because it can destroy you. It is not healthy and it is not safe to be upset about something but never talking about it. Whatever it is get it off of your chest and tell others how you feel.

Let's stop with the pity party and forgive, but not without working on forgiving yourself first. You may not forget, but you must forgive and move on. You really have not forgiven anyone, not even yourself, for dealing with that particular relationship or situation. It is simply called "out of sight, out of mind". If you do not see the person, then you will not think about them. Because you no longer see them, you sense a form of letting go; but, in actuality; you just put it to the back of your mind. This causes a reaction every time you see them, think of them, or think of the situation. It takes away from your energy; it is not healthy, and it causes sickness to form within your body. The Bible simply says in Mark 11:25-26 that we cannot be forgiven unless we forgive others. This is a great principle to live by and to honor.

Most times it will take a lot of prayer, tears and most importantly understanding, but it will be worth it all because you cannot stay mad at yourself forever. Once you have forgiven yourself, then work on forgiving that person and/or situation because you do not want your un-forgiveness to turn into bitterness and hate. Lastly, after you have forgiven, pray and ask God to forgive you!

PRAYER

Lord, forgiveness is so hard for me, and, although I don't want to hold on to things, I find myself doing so. I don't want to be bitter and angry; help me to forgive. I need to first start by forgiving myself. Lord, help me to forgive myself and to love myself without feeling rejected. I want to ask for forgiveness from you, Lord; and, most importantly, I want to forgive those that have come against me. I want to move past it; I want my heart to be free and full of love and forgiveness. Help me to release the fear, the hurt, the pain, and the rejection as I trust in you.

In Jesus mighty name.

Amen.

CONCLUSION

This book was written to help the many women that are just like I used to be: stuck in a bad headspace within their marriage, and unsure of how to cope. I made it through it all, but it was a hard road to discover on my own. I knew that with God all things were and are possible, and even though I lost my way and needed to be reminded of who God was, I always prayed. I am now dedicating myself to helping women that need help in order to find themselves again, in order for them to find their voice again. Sometimes all it takes is knowing that you are not alone on this journey of love.

There are many people going through silent heartbreak, pain and depression because they feel that they have no one to talk to, or no one that will understand them. Trust me, I totally get it. I have been there while people wondered why I continued to stay in a broken marriage for so long. I had nothing to show for it except my three girls. I had gotten married for better and for worse, and six out of the nine years made up the worst of my marriage. I could no longer take the deceit and mistrust. I had to break free for my sanity. I was completely lost. I was utterly broken and devastated because I thought it was love, I thought it was forever; I thought that he would honor and cherish me like our vows said. Because I had a hard time believing that those vows were all lies, it took a lot of prayer, deliverance, and coming back into my right mind for me to find myself again and for me to find my way back to reality. God had to give me a strategy in order for me to come to the realization that it was time for me to pick up and move on with my life. When only one person wants to fix a marriage, it will never work and that was the long, hard lesson that I had to endure for many years.

Sometimes in life we have to know when enough is enough. This may include knowing when the arguing and fighting need to change. Knowing how and when to help yourself inside of your relationship, knowing how to get help for your relationship, and knowing how to communicate effectively with your man. It is imperative that you find the strength to pray for that man especially when going through hard times and the good times as well. Instead of arguing all of the time, be still you will learn that your husband is not your enemy all he needs is for you to pray for him, your relationship, and pray for yourself.

Proverbs 31:10- talks about a virtuous women, it talks about how the woman builds up her husband and prays for him. She takes care of home making sure her husband and children are well taken care of. They do not need to ask her for anything because she makes their clothing, she prepares their food, she is an entrepreneur, and she is the back bone of the family all while treating her husband like a King. This does not go unnoticed because her family shows how much they appreciate her, love her, and respect her, her family calls her blessed. They have respect and honor for one another and inside of their household is nothing but peace. The peace that the woman brings to the home by making sure that the house is ran smoothly all while working her 9 to 5. God, I wish I would have had the chance to meet this Proverbs 31 woman that is described in the Bible because at times it can get really rough. It can become draining trying to hold down the house, uplift your man, make his clothing, the children clothing, taking care of home while still working a job and have a hustle on the side. Sometimes it seems impossible to hold it all in and keep it all together. This is where prayer come in, faith, and believing that God will show you the way if you are going through a tough time.

Regardless of your situation, please know that you will rediscover love again maybe it is self-love that you are looking for. You may rediscover it in your current relationship or even in a new one. Take me as an example. My fiancé has taught me so much about love and myself. He has taught me how to live and love again. I am truly grateful for him showing me the light again as I am now able to help other women be bold and strong through prayer, faithfulness, and most of all love. I hope you soon will be able to do the same. God bless!

An Unnecessary Breakdown Within Your Relationship

PRAYER

Father, I am coming to you and asking that you help heal the souls and hearts that have been broken. I place them at your feet and ask that you lead them, and guide them to recovery. Lead us all, Jesus! I ask that you bless each and every person that read this book, I pray that you touch their souls. Guide them into the right direction for their lives. I pray that they use the words and prayers out of this book and apply it to their lives in order to live a more peaceful life. I thank you Father for your wisdom that you have placed on the inside of me in order to reach the people that need you the most. We love you, Lord.

In Jesus Mighty Name I Pray. Amen.

www.ingramcontent.com/pod-product-compliance
Lightning Source LLC
Chambersburg PA
CBHW060222050426
42446CB00013B/3143